PRAYING
through your
DIVORCE

PRAYING
through your
DIVORCE

Karen O'Donnell

ST. ANTHONY MESSENGER PRESS
Cincinnati, Ohio

Library of Congress Cataloging-in-Publication Data

O'Donnell, Karen, 1954—
  Praying through your divorce / by Karen O'Donnell.
    p. cm.
  ISBN 0-86716-494-8 (pbk.)
  1. Divorced people—Prayer-books and devotions—
  English. 2. Divorce—Religious aspects—Catholic
  Church—Prayer-books and devotions—English.
  3. Catholic Church—Prayer-books and devotions—
  English.
I. Title.
  BX2170.D5 O36 2002
  242'.846—dc21

                                            2002014661

Cover and book design by Mark Sullivan

ISBN 0-86716-494-8

Published by St. Anthony Messenger Press
Printed in the U.S.A.
www.AmericanCatholic.org

For my children, Ryan and Meghan . . .
I love you bigger than the sky!

Contents

Prayer for: Acceptance 1

Affirmation 2

Answers 3

Art 4

Beginnings 5

Blessings 6

Books 7

Challenges 8

My Children 9

Clarity 10

Closure 11

Compassion 12

Confidence 13

Courage 14

This Day 15

Direction 16

Energy 17

Everything 18

My Ex-Spouse 19

Faith 20

Fun 21

Friends 22

Prayer for: The Future 23

Gentleness 24

God's Will 25

A Good Day 26

Good News 27

Gratitude 28

Healing 29

Our Home 30

Hope 31

Joy 32

Keepsakes 33

Laughter 34

Light 35

Listening 36

Little Things 37

Love 38

Me 39

Mealtimes 40

Memories 41

This Minute 42

Music 43

Organization 44

Prayer for: Paperwork 45

Patience 46

Peace 47

A Positive Outlook 48

Possibilities 49

Priorities 50

Questions 51

Relief 52

Self-Acceptance 53

Sleep 54

Softness 55

Solitude 56

Strength 57

Support People 58

Tears 59

Time 60

Trust 61

Truth 62

Understanding 63

Wisdom 64

No one who gets married expects to end up
divorced. I certainly did not expect to see the
end of my "lifetime" commitment. But divorce is
a painful reality.

Divorce is never easy on anyone, no matter how
simple or complicated the reasons are, or how
easy or difficult the process is. Only someone
who has personally experienced it can truly have
insight into the emotional, psychological and
spiritual trial of this journey. Family and friends
might sympathize and be supportive but, unless
they have lived through it themselves, they
cannot fully comprehend the pain of it. Certainly
divorce touches many lives—friends and family,
coworkers and neighbors—but none so much as
those who are divorcing and their children.

This book is the result of my own journey
through divorce. My faith has given me the
strength to endure and the hope for a future of
possibilities. These prayers seem to have been a

gift from God's hand. They encompass the many feelings that are part of divorce. There will be many tears, frustrations and pain with each divorce. But God is always with us—a quiet, inner, encouraging voice, an invisible arm around our shoulders—gently guiding us toward a happier future.

I truly believe that everything does indeed happen for a reason. I hope these prayers speak to you and enable you to speak to God as well. God can ease our pain and show us there is an abundance of light at the end of this path!

I hope that your struggles are few, and your joys are many!

—Karen O'Donnell

ACKNOWLEDGMENTS

My deepest thanks to my wonderful friends and
family who have helped me make it through,
and a special thank-you to Katie, my editor,
for everything she's done.

Prayer for Acceptance

Dear God,

I am working on acceptance.

Sometimes it is difficult to accept the hard
moments in my life.

But I know there are many things I cannot
change,

so I must learn to accept them.

I must learn to embrace reality

and welcome it as a series of challenges.

Please help me to accept the things I must.

Let me not hide from fear but walk firmly

in the light of my faith.

Help me to believe that I can get through

all of this

if I face it,

accept it

and do whatever I can to make things better.

I pray for the grace, and the freedom, that
acceptance will bring me.

PRAYER FOR AFFIRMATION

Dear God,

I feel rejected today.

I feel hurt by people's words and actions.

I feel so much less than the wonderful human
being you created me to be.

Please help me to pause, to pray,

to think about all the people in my life
who accept me unconditionally.

Help me to remember that you, too,

accept all of us,

all of your children, unconditionally.

What better love can there be than that?

Please help me to let go of my rejected feelings
and hurt ego

and focus instead on the loving, accepting
people in my life.

Thank you for your unconditional love,

which has no boundaries, no limits!

PRAYER FOR ANSWERS

Dear God,

I have plenty of questions in my life,

but I am short on answers.

With the issues I face,

I seek to resolve as many things as I can.

Help me listen to the answers you offer me.

Give me courage when the answers I get

are not the ones I want.

Help me realize that I will not always like the
  answers I get,

but they will be what's best for me.

I pray not only for the answers to my questions,

but for the courage to really listen to them,

to really hear them,

and to act on them, too!

Dear God,

Thank you for art.

I feel peace when I walk through a museum.

I am uplifted by the images, the colors,

the spirit and the passion I see there.

I am moved to hopeful visions for my own life.

I am also inspired by the artwork of my
children.

The creative spirit I find there is so open and
fresh,

so alive,

just like the children themselves.

Help me to cultivate and express my own artistic
spirit,

whether through artwork

or a creative meal.

Let me feed my creativity and inspire others,

as they have inspired me.

Thank you, God, for art!

Prayer for Beginnings

Dear God,

I pray for beginnings,

new beginnings,

for my children and me.

I pray for a new start for us —

a clean, fresh piece of paper

on which to write life's next chapter.

I pray for springtime

to ease the winter sorrow in my heart.

I pray for the wisdom to cherish

these new beginnings.

Prayer for Blessings

Dear God,
Thank you for all your blessings:
for the health of my children and my own
    health,
for the awareness that I have all that I really
    need today.
I give thanks that I do not want as much as I
    once did,
that I am starting to value what is truly
    important.
I thank you for all kinds of weather—
sweet sun, soft snow, fresh rain.
I thank you for the gift of hope.
I thank you for my friends, my family and my
    work.
I thank you for food on my table and a warm
    place to sleep.
I thank you mostly for the faith that keeps me
    going,
the belief that you are a good and kind God
who will guide all of us through our troubles.
For small joys I thank you, too:
the laughter my children and I share,
a quiet moment to myself,
the sun streaming in the window.
For all these blessings,
I thank you.

PRAYER FOR BOOKS

Dear God,

Thank you for so many uplifting books.

They have become a source of spiritual food
for me.

They give me not only wisdom,

but a sense of respite in days of turmoil.

They bring joy and relaxation to me

and, yes, even a badly needed escape for just a
little while.

Thank you for all the talented writers

and those responsible for filling my life with
books.

Thank you for enabling them to share their
passions,

their insights, their comforting words.

Thank you for the pleasure I get from reading
these books.

PRAYER FOR CHALLENGES

Dear God,

I do not want to thank you for all the challenges
    in my life,

but I will.

I do not like the obstacles in my life right now,

but I pray for your help

and realize that every challenge I face

will bring me closer to you.

Every challenge

will make my spirit stronger

and will make me a more understanding person.

These challenges will enable me

to help other people more effectively.

They will allow me

to be more compassionate with others

and more effective in handling the problems I
    face.

Help me realize that these challenges are not
    only about me.

They strengthen me and help me to be kinder
    and more loving with others.

Thank you for the challenges in my life.

Prayer for My Children

Dear God,

I pray for my children.

Keep them safe in your loving embrace.

Shelter them from any angry, hurtful words

they may hear about this divorce.

Help them know it is not their fault.

Help them to make their peace with all of this.

Do not let them be afraid or become bitter.

Let them still believe in the beauty of love.

Let them not doubt its value, even though they

have seen its failure.

Let them know how much I love them.

Let them feel this love.

Let them experience your great love and graces.

Dear God,

I pray for clarity.

I pray that the confusing and muddled picture of
my life

will become crisp and clear.

I pray for the answers I seek to become
apparent.

My life right now is a dark, muddy sky

which hides so much of what I need to know.

Help me find the clarity I need.

Let the vision be bright and powerful enough to
pierce this darkness.

And, if you grant me this clarity,

do not let me be afraid of what I see.

Though the answers may not be the ones I want,

let me trust they are the ones I need.

PRAYER FOR CLOSURE

Dear God,

I pray for a sense of closure with this divorce.

I know it will take time, but closure is something
   I need.

It will be difficult to achieve, I know.

We spent so many years together as a couple.

But I pray for and need the peace that closure
   will bring.

I need to feel comfortable with these endings in
   my life,

so that I may face the future with a smile.

Help me achieve this sense of closure,

so that I may put anxieties to rest and move
   forward

in a dance of joyous beginnings.

Dear God,

If I have learned one thing through this pain,

it is compassion.

It is so true that you never really know how a
person feels

unless you have lived through what they have.

I feel that way now.

I never realized the pain and loneliness divorce
could inflict on a person.

I could never have even imagined it.

I thought I knew how it would be, but I didn't.

It goes so much deeper than I knew.

It holds a pain that is palpable.

I know now that it takes experiencing something
firsthand

to really have compassion for another human
being.

Perhaps that is one great gift that has come
because of this divorce —

compassion for others.

Help me to use this compassion to guide others,

as so many others have kindly guided me.

PRAYER FOR CONFIDENCE

Dear God,

I pray for the confidence I need at my job.

Let me shake off any doubts and insecurities I
have.

Let me instead smile faithfully

with certainty that I am doing the best possible
job I can.

It is difficult to do this when I feel so vulnerable
inside, so afraid.

So I ask your help in feeling confident

so that I can do the best possible job

of supporting my children and myself.

Give me total confidence, too, in my personal
life.

Let me feel I am a worthwhile, lovable person
deserving of good things in my life.

I pray for confidence.

Prayer for Courage

Dear God,

I am afraid.

I am afraid of so many things right now,

especially the future —

that great black unknown.

I am afraid of making the wrong decisions.

I am afraid of what might happen to all of us

    because of this divorce.

Please help me to be brave.

Give me the courage I need to face my fears

and walk with you down the path I must follow.

Light my way with faith,

warm me with love

and nourish me with hope.

Prayer for This Day

Dear God,

I pray just to get through this one day.

Help me not to worry about an uncertain future,

about what may happen tomorrow.

Help me to find a way to focus

on the moment I am living right now.

Help me to find a bit of peace in this day, a bit

of joy.

Let me worry only about living this day,

just this day,

this gift you have given me.

PRAYER FOR DIRECTION

Dear God,

I need a spiritual map today.

I need to know what direction to take in my life.

My mind is cluttered with a million possibilities.

Please help me to quiet my mind

so I can see more clearly what your path is

    for me.

Help me to follow the path I was meant to

    travel.

Give me courage, and let me know

that you walk down this path with me.

Prayer for Energy

Dear God,

Please energize me in all ways—

physically, emotionally and spiritually.

Help me to take good care of my body

so that I am strong and healthy enough

to care for my children

and do all the work I must do.

Help me to be strong emotionally.

The process of divorce and starting a new life is
    all so draining,

sometimes I feel I'll never make it through.

Help me to let my feelings out gently,

so they do not hurt anyone else.

Help me to be as strong as an oak but as flexible
    as a willow.

Help me to be spiritually powerful.

Let me hold fast to my faith,

It is my lifeboat in these turbulent times.

It has gotten me through tough times before.

I know that it will help me survive these
    days, too.

So please energize me in all these ways!

PRAYER FOR EVERYTHING

Dear God,
Thank you for everything,
for all of my present blessings
and for those yet to come!

PRAYER FOR MY EX-SPOUSE

Dear God,

I pray for my ex-spouse

to find a way to your heart.

Though we will no longer be husband and wife,

we once shared a great love and respect for one
   another.

I still care about this person as a human being

and as one of your children.

Help this child of yours to find peace and joy

and let me find forgiveness.

Dear God,

Let me not lose faith.

It is hard to believe in joy

in times of pain.

Let my faith be the light

that guides me through this darkness.

I know I am your child and you love me.

Do not let me lose sight of this.

Help me to keep praying and believing that we
will be OK,

that we will all get through this.

Help me to believe that our lives will be better.

Help me keep my faith strong.

Prayer for Friends

Dear God,

I thank you for my friends.

I don't know what I did to deserve such
treasured people in my life,

but you must love me very much to surround me
with them.

I am grateful for their love and support.

I am moved by their caring,

their perceptions and their patience.

I wonder how they can be so patient with me!

Even when I share my pain and confusion,

still they do not turn away from me.

They stay with me.

They listen.

They love.

They accept all of me—joy and pain, good
and bad.

They remain a constant, loving reminder
of the goodness in all people.

They give me hope for my future.

They give wings to my dreams.

Thank you for these treasured friends!

Dear God,

My kids tell me I'm no fun anymore.

I know that must be true.

Sometimes I focus only on the problems—

there is so much I must handle on my own now!

I try to explain to them how many

responsibilities I have,

but they're still children after all.

Let me make time to have fun.

Whether it is a board game, an indoor picnic

or tossing them a ball.

Let me make an effort to have some fun.

They need more joy in their lives right now,

and so do I.

Prayer for The Future

Dear God,

I pray today for the future—

that blank, looming thing that scares me so.

Help me to look at it not as a fearful, black

   place,

but as a light-filled sky, a hopeful place.

Let me see it as a surprise package to unwrap,

something that will hold much joy and delight.

As today is surely a gift,

do not let me be afraid of the future,

but to see it, too, as a present.

PRAYER FOR GENTLENESS

Dear God,

Today I pray for the hardest taskmaster
in my life: me!

I can be my own worst enemy.

The one who's never satisfied with my work and
my accomplishments is me!

The one who blames me for everything is me!

Help me to stop being so tough on myself and to
be realistic in my expectations.

Help me to give myself a break once in a while.

Help me to give myself permission to take time
for me

or to do something special for myself.

Most of all, help me to be gentle with myself,

to love myself as much as I love those dear
to me,

so that I can love them more fully.

Help me to be gentle with myself and love
myself more!

PRAYER FOR GOD'S WILL

Dear God,

I pray for what you know is the highest good.

I have to be honest when I say I am afraid of
what the highest good is.

It may mean more pain ahead for me

before I taste the happiness and peace for which
I long.

Help me to be strong, committed and earnest
in my prayer for what is best for me and my
children.

Let me give myself completely in a spirit of trust

as I pray for what you deem best.

You know much better than I

what is really the highest good.

Help me trust in you without question, without
fear.

Help me quiet my spirit,

calm my confusions

and walk joyously along the path

you have cleared for me.

PRAYER FOR A GOOD DAY

Dear God,

Thank you for this full, rich day.

Though it has been hectic and exhausting,

I truly felt alive today.

I felt like I made a difference with all that I did.

Thank you, too, for the energy you gave me to
   get through this day,

for my healthy, vital body and strong mind.

This teaches me that if I get through the bad
   days,

I'll get to a good day eventually.

That day was today!

Prayer for Good News

Dear God,

Thank you for some good news today.

I have needed some.

Some days bring only bad news and more
problems,

so I am even more grateful for these bits of good
news.

They give me courage and hope,

in this frightening, uncertain time.

Good news is like a springtime day in the middle
of winter,

a balm for my soul!

PRAYER FOR GRATITUDE

Dear God,

It is hard to have an attitude of gratitude.

I am finding it easier to feel sorry for myself,

to pity myself for the state of my life right now.

Please help me to cultivate a new gratitude.

Let me constantly be aware of all the things in
my life

for which I should be grateful:

family, friends, my health and the health of those
I love,

my faith, the knowledge that I am never really
alone,

that you are always here with me.

For that I am most grateful, God,

that you are here with me!

Prayer for Healing

Dear God,

I pray for healing today.

My spirit is battered.

Sometimes I feel so much emotional pain

that I don't think I can bear it.

Let me feel your gentle love washing over me,

cleansing my spiritual wounds and healing me.

Help me feel stronger each day.

Let me look to that day in the future

when the pain is not so intense

but rather a faint memory.

Please heal me, God.

Prayer for Our Home

Dear God,

Ease my concerns about where we will live.

Let me remember that our home is wherever we
are as a family.

The size of the house does not matter,

the size of the hearts that live there does.

I love my family.

Help them feel safe and content wherever we
live.

Help them feel the warmth of love deep in their
hearts.

Do not let us worry about where we will live,

but reassure us that we will live there together
in love.

Prayer for Hope

Dear God,

Help me to hold on to hope.

It is difficult sometimes.

But I know that no matter how bad things get,

there is always hope.

It is one of your greatest gifts.

Help me to keep this hope

and realize that there is a better life ahead.

Dear God,

Help me today to celebrate.

Help me to celebrate me!

Help me to be proud of my accomplishments
and to delight in my dreams and plans for the
future.

Help me to accept all of me —
my good points and bad.

Let me cherish myself
for the unique person I am —
a one-of-a-kind creation
made by the greatest artist — you!

Help me to truly experience joy today
and to see myself as a special gift to the world.

Let me make the world a better place by being
here.

PRAYER FOR KEEPSAKES

Dear God,

I don't know how to feel about our family
    photographs and keepsakes.

They are bittersweet.

I look through these mementoes of happy times
    and my eyes fill with tears.

I wonder what happened to these good times.

I feel painfully sad for the state of our lives today.

Help me keep these happy memories in my heart.

Give me the strength to look at these lovely things,

and memories of lovely times

and remember them for what they are—

treasured pieces of my life.

Just because my today is filled with pain,

doesn't mean I can't look with fondness

    on bits of my past.

So I pray for your help

to ease my sadness as I look at these pictures.

Let me smile at the warmth I find there.

Let it help melt away some of the sorrow I feel.

PRAYER FOR LAUGHTER

Dear God,

I pray for some laughter in my life.

Help me lighten my life.

Let the music of laughter be shared by my
   children and me.

Let us find a few brief moments of respite

in this all-too-serious world of divorce.

Let me stop being serious long enough

to free my spirit in laughter

and pure delight!

PRAYER FOR LIGHT

Dear God,

I pray for light.

I pray to come out of this despair and into your
light.

I pray for all kinds of light —

not only sunlight, starlight, moonlight —

but the light of hope, the light of joy, the light of
love.

I pray for the light of faith

to guide me through this blackest of all tunnels.

I pray for the light of wisdom

to shine as a beacon down this dark path.

I pray for your light!

Prayer for Listening

Dear God,

Help me to listen more and talk less.

Help me really hear what my children are telling
  me —

not just by what they say,

but also by what they don't say.

Help me take time to think about their actions

before I respond in anger.

Let me listen more to my heart,

my intuition, my feelings.

I need to listen less to outside voices

and more to my inner voice.

Open my spirit, too,

so that I may truly listen to your word,

and your plans for me.

Help me to quiet my questions.

Help me to be patient,

while your words settle into my soul.

Help me to listen.

PRAYER FOR LITTLE THINGS

Dear God,

Help me to remember

all the little things that give me joy.

I find it so hard to remember joy

when I am beset by troubles.

Let me give thanks for the health of my

   children,

for their smiles,

for their hugs and kisses.

Let me give thanks for the weather—

all of it—snow, rain and sun.

Let me feel grateful to be alive to experience

   each kind of weather.

I give thanks, too, for trees, flowers, lakes,

rivers, oceans, birds and creatures of every kind,

   and for every bit of nature you made for us to

   take pleasure in.

For music, for art, for good books,

a cup of tea in the morning.

Thank you, God, for each little thing

that helps to brighten my life

in dark times.

PRAYER FOR LOVE

Dear God,

I want to believe in love.

Please help me to believe love still exists,

that a sweet love is possible for me someday.

Let me not become bitter because of this
  experience.

Let me still believe in the miracle of love.

I know you wish it for all of your children.

Prayer for Me

Dear God,

Thank you for the person I see each day in the
   mirror.

Though I try to smile at this face I see,

it isn't always possible.

At night in loneliness I sometimes cry

and see the tears streak my cheeks.

But this is only a moment in my life,

I know it will pass.

And the next day I get up and smile at myself,

secure in the fact that I am hopeful and alive

and you are here with me.

Thank you for my mirror,

for the chance to see myself as others see me,

and for the faith to see myself as you see me.

Help me to be the person you created me to be.

PRAYER FOR MEALTIMES

Dear God,

Help us take time together as a family.

Though our mealtimes may be short and few,

let us cherish each other's company and share

   each other's love.

Let us talk to each other —

actually talk to each other —

and listen more, too.

Let us celebrate our meal times

as a chance to be together in love.

PRAYER FOR MEMORIES

Dear God,

Help me to keep and cherish

the good memories of my marriage.

Help me remember the joys, both great and
small.

Let them remain the jewels that they are.

Do not let this divorce diminish them

or erase them from my memory.

So, too, let the bad memories go.

Do not let them poison my life.

Let me sift them through my fingers

like the finest grains of sand.

Let me hold onto the good memories instead,

keeping them in my hands, my heart,

as the jewels that they are.

PRAYER FOR THIS MINUTE

Dear God,

Time has become so important.

I pray for your help to get through just this one
minute.

One day at a time often seems like too big a
chunk to me,

too much to handle when life is so
overwhelming.

Be with me in just this minute.

Help me live gracefully through it till I reach the
next one.

Help me to remember that we do indeed live our
lives

one breath at a time.

And so I pray for this minute, God.

PRAYER FOR MUSIC

Dear God,

Thank you for music.

It has become an important part of my day.

There are songs so sweet, so sad,

they open up my emotions and give me

  permission to cry.

There are songs so light, so hopeful,

they inspire me with the joyful possibilities in

  my life.

Music is helping to ease my burdens.

Thank you for all the talented people

responsible for bringing music into my life.

Prayer for Organization

Dear God,

I pray for your help to be better organized.

I feel like everything is piling up and getting
away from me.

The house is a mess.

There is so much paperwork and so many
obligations

I run out of time at the end of the day!

It seems my life is a mountain of tasks left
undone.

Please help me to become more organized.

Help me to learn to break down the
overwhelming tasks

into tiny chunks that I can handle.

Help me to do what I can in each day

and be comfortable and satisfied with whatever
I've accomplished.

Help me to concentrate not on all the things left
undone,

but on everything I've done for the day.

Help me to manage my time and my life as
effectively as I can,

but let me remember that the loving things I do
each day for myself, my family and my friends
will be remembered much longer

than whether my kitchen is spotless!

Prayer for Paperwork

Dear God,

I have never heard of a prayer for paperwork,

but I am praying it right now.

Please give me the strength and means for

handling all of it:

legal documents, bills, forms.

Give me the eye for detail I need.

Give me the wisdom necessary to be successful.

Give me the patience I need to deal with the

mess of all this.

If it is possible, please bless all of this

paperwork.

PRAYER FOR PATIENCE

Dear God,
Please give me the patience I need
to get through this divorce.
I need patience to respond with love to my
children.
I know they are confused and angry,
but they know how to push my buttons.
I can feel my patience ebbing out of me.
Please give me the extra patience I need with
them.
Help me deal with them lovingly and kindly.
Give me the patience, too, to deal with my ex-
spouse.
Let me realize that whatever happened,
we both did the best we could do with what we
had.
Also give me the patience I need
to get through all the time it will take for this
painful process.
I want to just snap my fingers and make it all be
over,
but I know I cannot.
Please give me the patience I need for all of this.

Prayer for Peace

Dear God,

I pray not to become bitter because of this
   divorce.

It seems so easy to feel this way.

Help me to fight this feeling

which can only destroy any inner sense of peace
   and hope.

Help me instead to see life as a challenge.

Let me see my trials as a test of courage

and a means of adding strength to my spirit.

Do not let me not be bitter but rather help me
   seek to better my life.

Let me keep hope, faith and love as dear friends,

close to my heart and ever in my life.

PRAYER FOR A POSITIVE OUTLOOK

Dear God,

I need your help in refraining from self-pity.

Please help me not to concentrate on all the
negative things.

Help me instead to know how lucky I am,

how fortunate and blessed I am,

to have wonderful family and friends to support
me.

Pity is a draining thing.

It robs my soul of joy, courage and peace.

Help me to keep my blessings close and my self-
pity far away.

Let me choose to face my life instead,

with a prayer in my heart and a smile in my
eyes.

Prayer for Possibilities

Dear God,

Help me keep in mind the possibilities in my life.

Let me think beyond the limits of my life as it is

at this moment.

Let me remember that there are as many

possibilities for me

as there are grains of sand on the beach.

Let me know that both are endless.

Help me to seek out these new possibilities

and choose those that will be best for me and

best serve you.

PRAYER FOR PRIORITIES

Dear God,

Help me to slow down.

I feel like I am racing ahead,

trying to solve a lifetime of problems in one day.

Help me to ease it all down to a simmer, instead
of a rolling boil.

I need to learn to concentrate on one problem at
a time.

Help me learn to prioritize better.

Help me to learn how to let some things go.

Let me realize that some of my problems can
wait.

Please help me to slow down

and take care of the important things first.

PRAYER FOR QUESTIONS

Dear God,

Why should I pray for questions?

You've given me too many to cope with right
  now anyway!

I don't want any more!

What I do want, though, is an appreciation of all
  these questions.

They are all like bits of clay

that my hands will form into a spectacular
  vessel —

a vessel to hold the answers

that will form the masterpiece which is to be my
  life.

I offer this very vessel.

I am brim-filled with questions

which are being answered very, very slowly

with your patient, loving, creative hands!

Let me realize that I am richer in spirit

for the questions which are ever molding me.

Prayer for Relief

Dear God,

Please see fit to ease my burdens.

I have done my best

with the crosses I have had to bear.

Please lighten my load and bring more joy into
   my life.

If more joy is not possible,

then please give me the

strength to deal with all I must face.

Keep me hopeful.

Give me the faith I need to go on.

Keep me mindful of the small joys and

many blessings in my life.

I pray for your continued help on this difficult
   journey.

Prayer for Self-Acceptance

Dear God,

Help me to be patient for love.

Help me to realize that I will not find love

by seeking it desperately,

but love will find me

once I am comfortable and content with myself.

Let me learn to love myself first,

before I expect another person to love me.

Let me appreciate who I am —

both my strengths and weaknesses,

the good and bad in me,

my courage and my fears.

Let me be comfortable with this person I am

coming to know.

Let me love both the child and adult in me.

Let me learn to delight in who I am.

Let me love myself!

Prayer for Sleep

Dear God,

Tonight I pray for sleep.

I need some hours of peace

when both my mind and body are at rest.

This divorce process is painful

and seemingly endless.

I need to get some sleep

to help energize me for what tomorrow brings.

I am having trouble sleeping—

my mind cannot quiet itself.

Instead, all the worries, fears

and endless questions dance for hours,

keeping me awake.

I am exhausted from lack of sleep.

Please help me to settle my body and spirit.

Let soft dreams pillow my weary heart

and give me rest for just a little while.

Help ease my worries.

Fill my mind instead with tranquil lullabies of

   hope and peace

and sweet love.

Be with me tonight, God, and help me to sleep.

PRAYER FOR SOFTNESS

Dear God,

I pray for softness in my life.

My days are filled with the hard edges of bitter
  feelings,

mistrust and disillusionment.

They are filled with the sharpness of anger.

I pray for the fluffy comforts I need:

the hug of a child,

a special gift I buy just for me,

cuddling up with a book and tea for company,

remembering the warmth of my friendships

and the tranquility I get through accepting
  whatever befalls me.

I pray today for your love to envelop me like a
  warm blanket

keeping the biting cold away for just a little
  while.

Dear God,

Let me feel the warm light of your love

helping me to get through this loneliness.

I feel so isolated, so very alone.

I miss the constant companionship I once had.

I used to love time to myself, but it was different
   then.

That was a brief respite in a different life.

I have such an ache when I see husbands and
   wives together
      or parents and children.

When I hear of anniversary celebrations,

I cry to myself for what I have lost.

Please help me through these lonely times.

Please help me to try to use this time alone

to gain something —

spiritual strength,

an appreciation for myself as a person,

maybe even to develop a skill or talent I never
   had time for before.

Help me also realize

that I am never completely alone.

You are with me as I walk this path.

Prayer for Strength

Dear God,

Give me the strength I need on this journey.

Please help me to keep a seed of joy in my heart

and a smile of faith on my lips.

Let me believe, truly believe,

that I am doing what is right, what is best,

for my children and for myself.

Help me, I pray.

PRAYER FOR SUPPORT PEOPLE

Dear God,
I pray for all those people
helping us through these troubling times:
our priests, teachers, family, friends,
therapists, lawyers, mediators, doctors—
everyone involved.
They are trying to help us get through all this.
Give them strength.
Bless them and the important work they do
    for us and others.

Prayer for Tears

Dear God,

These days I have become a connoisseur of
 tears.

I spend so much time crying over my past,

my present and my future.

Going through a divorce makes you feel so
 much you have never felt before.

Please let me be grateful for my tears.

Let me realize they are an honest expression of
 my feelings.

My feelings are a treasured part of me —

let me remember that!

Help me to see my tears as a spiritual cleansing.

Let me see my tears not as a sign of weakness,

but of strength.

Let me realize they are a healing part of this
 process.

Be with me when I am tearful and vulnerable.

Wrap me in your loving arms,

and help me find peace in these tears

and a release from pain.

Prayer for Time

Dear God,

Help me realize that it's OK to take a little time
for me.

The stress is so great, I need a break.

Help me care for myself when I am weary,

with no guilt or shame for doing so.

I must be strong.

I know I can be strong with your help.

I know I can function better

with just a little time for me.

Help me to take this time.

Prayer for Trust

Dear God,

Help me to have complete trust in you.

Help me to trust that this time in my life is your will.

Help me to believe that there is something better in store for me.

It has become so hard for me to trust.

I have been hurt by trusting the wrong people.

I am sorry that this sometimes makes me doubt others who deserve my trust,

or even you!

Please help me to believe in your will without question.

Let me realize I do not walk completely alone,

for you are beside me all the way.

It is so easy for me to falter on this path,

to question and doubt.

Please help me to trust in you,

to believe in a better future for me,

even though I cannot see it now.

Dear God,

I seek the truth,

yet I am afraid of it, too.

I long to stop the game-playing people indulge
in,

life is too short to waste time.

But how can I stop others from their games?

Can I simply refuse to play along?

If I do stop playing, am I really prepared for the
truth?

I pray that I will be prepared,

that I am brave enough to see it

and face things as they truly are.

Even though the sun is too bright to look at
directly,

still it warms us deep within.

Truth is this bright, yet warming, too.

Give me the strength to face the truth

no matter how difficult it might be.

PRAYER FOR UNDERSTANDING

Dear God,

If I feel people judging me,

please stand by me.

Help me to realize that what I am doing

is in the best interests of my family.

Help me to be strong in the face of harsh

judgments

let them not sway me from the tasks I must do.

Be with me as I face these judgments.

Help me to know that your love is still with me,

gently guiding and protecting me.

PRAYER FOR WISDOM

Dear God,

I pray for wisdom.

I pray for the knowledge I need

to make the right decisions in my life right now.

Times are confusing

and it is difficult to clear my mind

so I can see the answers.

Give me the wisdom I need to hear the answers.

Wisdom is a clear, bright star in the blackest

sky.

Let me hold that star in my heart.

Please give me the strength I need to follow

through.